The SUMERIANS

Revised and Updated

JANE SHUTER

Heinemann Library
Chicago, Illinois

©2002, 2009 Heinemann Library
a division of Pearson Inc.
Chicago, Illinois

Customer Service 888-454-2279
Visit our website at www.heinemannraintree.com

Photo research by Mica Brancic
Designed by Richard Parker and Manhattan Design
Printed and bound in China by CTPS

13 12 11 10 09
10 9 8 7 6 5 4 3 2 1

New edition ISBNs: 978-1-4329-1331-1 (hardcover)
                      978-1-4329-1339-7 (paperback)

The Library of Congress has cataloged the first edition as follows:
Shuter, Jane.
The Sumerians / Jane Shuter.
p. cm. -- (History opens windows)
Includes bibliographical references and index.
Summary: Presents an overview of the ancient Sumerian culture,
discussing government, recreation, trade, travel, family life, food,
occupations, and entertainment.
ISBN 1-58810-592-X
1. Sumerians—Juvenile literature. [1. Sumerians.] I. Title. II.
Series.
DS72 .S56 2001
935'.0049995—dc21
                      2001004458

Acknowledgments
The author and publishers are grateful to the following for permission to reproduce copyright material: pp. 8, 25 © Scala/Art Resource; pp. 9, 11, 19 © Michael Holford; p. 10 © Bridgeman Art Library, Iraq Museum, Baghdad; p. 12 © Victor Boswell/National Geographic Society; pp. 13, 26 © Gianni Dagli Orti/Corbis; p. 14 © Georg Gerster/National Geographic Society; p. 16 © Nik Wheeler/Corbis; p. 20 © Courtesy of the Oriental Institute of the University of Chicago; p. 22 © Peter Willi/SuperStock; pp. 23, 30 © Erich Lessing/Art Resource; p. 24 © Burstein Collection/Corbis; pp. 28, 29 © British Museum/ Bridgeman Art Library.

Illustrations: p. 4 Eileen Mueller Neill; pp. 7, 17, 18, 21, 27 David Westerfield.
Cover photograph © 2003, Photo Scala Florence/HIP.

Contents

Some words are shown in bold, **like this**.
You can find out what they mean by looking in the glossary.

Introduction

The Sumerians lived in the fertile valley between the Euphrates and Tigris rivers in Asia. They lived in an area known as Mesopotamia, which means "the land between the rivers."

Tigris River

Euphrates River

Tel Asmar

Khafaje

Akshak

Sippar

AKKAD

Kish

Ancient course of river

Abu Salabikh

Nippur

Susa

Adab

Shoruppak

Umma

Ancient coastline

Uruk

Girsu

Lagash

Larsa

Ur

SUMER

Eridu

Desert

Persian Gulf

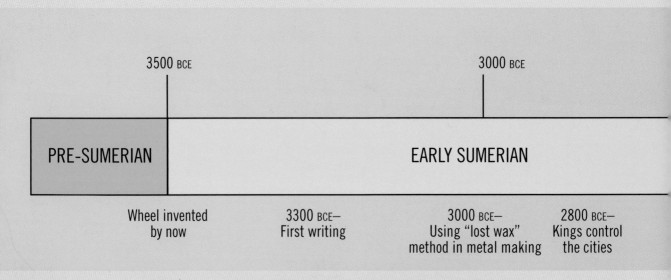

3500 BCE		3000 BCE	
PRE-SUMERIAN	EARLY SUMERIAN		
Wheel invented by now	3300 BCE— First writing	3000 BCE— Using "lost wax" method in metal making	2800 BCE— Kings control the cities

People first lived in Mesopotamia more than 9,000 years ago. In around 3500 BCE, the first Sumerians formed cities in the southern part of Mesopotamia. The two rivers often flooded in this area. The flooding left a rich soil that was good for farming. The Sumerians also built **canals** for **irrigation**.

Early Sumerians lived in **city-states**, each with its own king. People from different city-states often fought one another. This weakened their ability to fight outsiders. In about 2330 BCE, Akkadians from the north defeated the Sumerians. The Akkadians then governed a state together with the Sumerians. After that, Sumerian kings started to take over again.

In about 2125 BCE, the people of the **empire** of Ur rose up. They won control of Sumer. In 2004 BCE, a new wave of peoples fought the Sumerians. They destroyed Ur. It was the end of the Sumerian period.

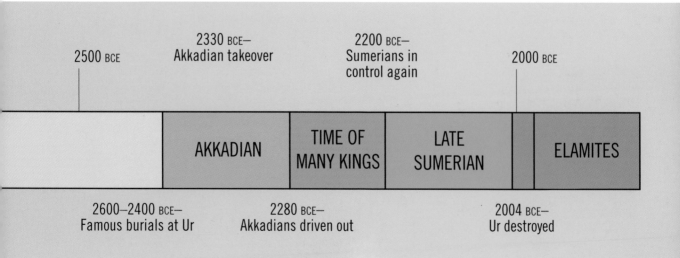

2500 BCE

2330 BCE—
Akkadian takeover

2200 BCE—
Sumerians in
control again

2000 BCE

AKKADIAN

TIME OF
MANY KINGS

LATE
SUMERIAN

ELAMITES

2600–2400 BCE—
Famous burials at Ur

2280 BCE—
Akkadians driven out

2004 BCE—
Ur destroyed

City-States

Each Sumerian **city-state** included a city and the land around it where farming took place. Each city was built around a **temple** known as a **ziggurat**. The Sumerians believed this was where gods lived.

Some city-states were bigger and more powerful than others. **Canals** or a river often marked the border of a city-state. Even so, the Sumerians often fought one another over the borders of a city-state.

The Sumerians did not have one single ruler. A different king ruled each city-state. Children of different kings might marry each other. This helped keep the peace between different city-states.

When they were not fighting, city-states traded with one another. Each city-state was organized in a similar way. All Sumerians spoke the same language. They used the same written language. They had the same religion.

This modern drawing of the city of Ur is based on what experts have discovered.

The ziggurat and other important buildings were in the middle of the city.

Ordinary people lived and worked around the edge of the city.

The city had mud brick walls for safety.

A river or canal often formed the border of a city-state.

How Were the Sumerians Ruled?

Historians think this bronze head of a king is Sargon, sometimes called Naram-Sin.

Early Sumerian cities were run by groups of men. They would choose a *patesi*, or "great man," to rule over them. Over the *patesi* ruled a *lugal*, or king, who was head of each **city-state**. The kings were also priests. Each king chose a city-state's next leader. Late in Sumerian times, kings ruled in families. The Sumerians believed that the god of their city-state chose their king.

Each city-state "belonged" to a different god. The city of Ur served Nanna, the moon god, while the city of Uruk served Inanna, the goddess of love and war. Each city had a large walled area in the middle where the **temples** were. The biggest temple was for the city's god. These walled areas also held storehouses and government buildings. The king ran the city-state for its god. His job was to keep the people well fed, the temples in good condition, and the city safe from outsiders.

This stone carving shows Ur Nanshe, ruler of Lagash in about 2480 BCE. He is carrying a basket of bricks on his head.

War

War was a part of Sumerian life. The **city-states** often fought each other. They also fought invaders from nearby countries who tried to take over. Each Sumerian city-state had its own army. The armies were not very big at first, but they were well-trained and had good weapons. The soldiers had metal-tipped spears, daggers, large shields, and leather armor. Sumerians are the first people we know of who used tactics (planned actions) such as attacking in a block marching in step.

This king's helmet made from silver and gold was too valuable to use in battle. But when they fought, kings wore metal helmets, not leather ones like their soldiers.

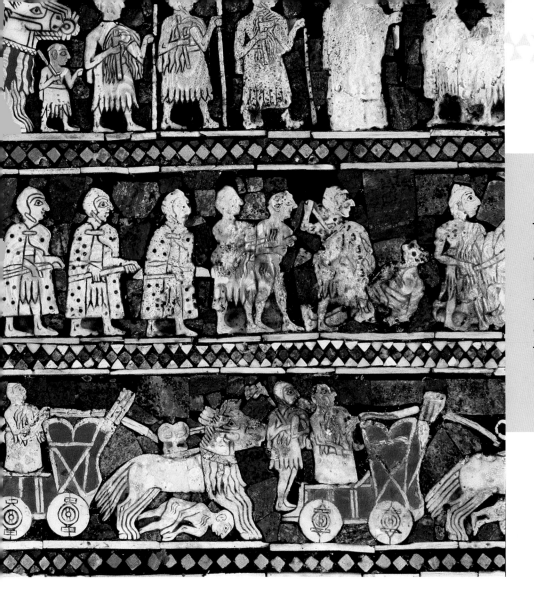

This picture shows an army going into battle. You can see the soldiers' armor and the chariots they used.

The Sumerians were the first people who we know used wheels. They used them to build carts and war chariots—small, horse-drawn vehicles. The chariots were useful for carrying weapons and shields as the army marched to war. They were also used for fighting. One man drove the chariot, while another stood behind the driver and threw spears at the enemy. Soldiers also used battle axes with long handles to fight from chariots. Daggers were used in hand-to-hand fighting.

Religion

These statues were left as offerings at Sumerian temples. The ones with big eyes are thought to be gods.

The Sumerians believed in many different gods and goddesses who controlled the weather, the flooding of the rivers, and almost all parts of everyday life. They worshipped these gods and goddesses at public **temples**, but also at smaller **shrines** in their own homes. Priests were very important because they were the link between the gods and the people. Religious **festivals** were held several times a month and on special days, such as the celebration of the New Year.

Sumerians believed that one of the gods protected each **city-state**. People prayed mainly to that god. However, they did not want the other gods to get jealous and harm the city, so they prayed to them, too. Each Sumerian also had a god as his or her own protector. They prayed to the god of the city about things that affected the city, such as a good **harvest**. If they were sick they prayed to their own god or goddess. The Sumerians believed in a life after death. They buried their dead with things they would need in the afterlife, such as clothes, furniture, and food.

The people who followed the Sumerians had many of the same gods and goddesses. Here is a Babylonian ruler, standing in front of the sun god.

Temples

Temples were an important part of Sumerian religion. Workers and **slaves** built temples from mud bricks on a mud brick platform. By 2000 BCE these temples had become **ziggurats**. Ziggurats have three platforms, one on top of the other, each smaller than the one below. At the top of the temple was a **shrine** where the god or goddess lived.

Priests visited the shrines every day to pray and leave offerings. Priestesses and musicians also worked in the temples. Some priests ran the religious activities of the temples. Others ran the day-to-day activities. This included listing all the crops grown to check that none had been damaged or destroyed.

This is a reconstruction of a ziggurat. The only entrance to a ziggurat was by the steep staircase in the center.

The shrine at the top was where the priests looked after statues of the gods.

This is the only set of stairs that lead straight to the shrine at the top.

The bottom layer of the ziggurat measured 205 feet (62 meters) by 141 feet (43 meters) and was 36 feet (11 meters) high.

Animals and offerings were brought as sacrifices on special days.

Travel and Trade

This silver model shows a Sumerian boat. Boats were used to travel along canals and rivers.

Ordinary Sumerians did not travel far from their **city-states**. It could be dangerous, because other city-states were not always friendly. But they did travel locally in several ways. Most people walked or rode donkeys. Donkeys were also used to carry heavy loads. The Sumerians used wheels, so they could also carry goods in carts. The system of rivers and **canals** in Mesopotamia meant that people could also travel by boat. Boats were especially useful for moving heavy things, such as loads of mud bricks, from place to place.

Sumerian traders traveled in order to trade grain and cloth for goods such as silver, shells, and decorative stones. They also traded for **bitumen** to use as mortar in buildings. Sumer was in a good place in the trade route system. Many of the goods the traders bought came from far away. But they often only had to go to the nearest big trading town to buy these things. If they did travel farther, they could buy things more cheaply and make more money.

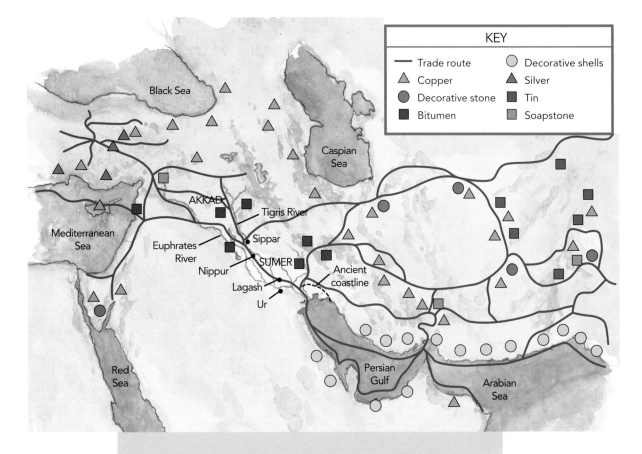

This map shows the most important trade routes for Sumerian merchants and the most important goods they wanted to buy.

Farming and Food

Farming was very important to the Sumerians. Each **city-state** had to grow enough food to feed its people. Most city-states tried to grow more grain than they needed. Then they could use the extra grain to trade for things they needed from other places.

Sumerian farmers used ponds and **canals** to control the water of the two rivers. They used several kinds of plows, as well as simple wooden tools. Grain was the most important crop. It could be made into flour, bread, beer, and porridge. There were special religious **ceremonies** for planting grain, but not for other crops.

The Sumerians invented a seed sowing machine, which could plant seeds more quickly and evenly than sowing by hand.

Sumerian farmers kept cattle, sheep, and goats.

Sumerian farmers also grew other crops, including beans, onions, garlic, lettuce, cucumbers, leeks, turnips, and mustard. Many plants were used by doctors to make **ointments** for treating illnesses. They also made **poultices** to stop infection by mixing plants and herbs, warming then, and then putting them on cuts.

Farmers raised cattle for milk and meat, and to use as work animals. They raised sheep and goats for milk, meat, and wool. Donkeys carried heavy loads. Sumerians turned animal skins into leather, which they used mainly for armor.

Houses

Sumerians who lived outside the city often lived in one-roomed reed huts, like the one shown here.

Many Sumerians lived in one-roomed houses made from mud brick. They had **reed** roofs and a hearth at one end for cooking. (The hearth is the area in front of a fireplace.) Homes were usually whitewashed inside and out. In these homes, people slept on beds with wooden frames, using rope stretched tightly across the frames to make the beds springy. Richer people had several rooms around a courtyard and sometimes even a second floor. In some cities there may have been a few three-story buildings. These would have been shared by several families.

People usually cooked over an open fire. They could cook their food in clay pots that sat in the flames, or they could roast it over the fire. Most people did not eat meat every day. They ate vegetables, cheese, and bread, and drank beer and milk.

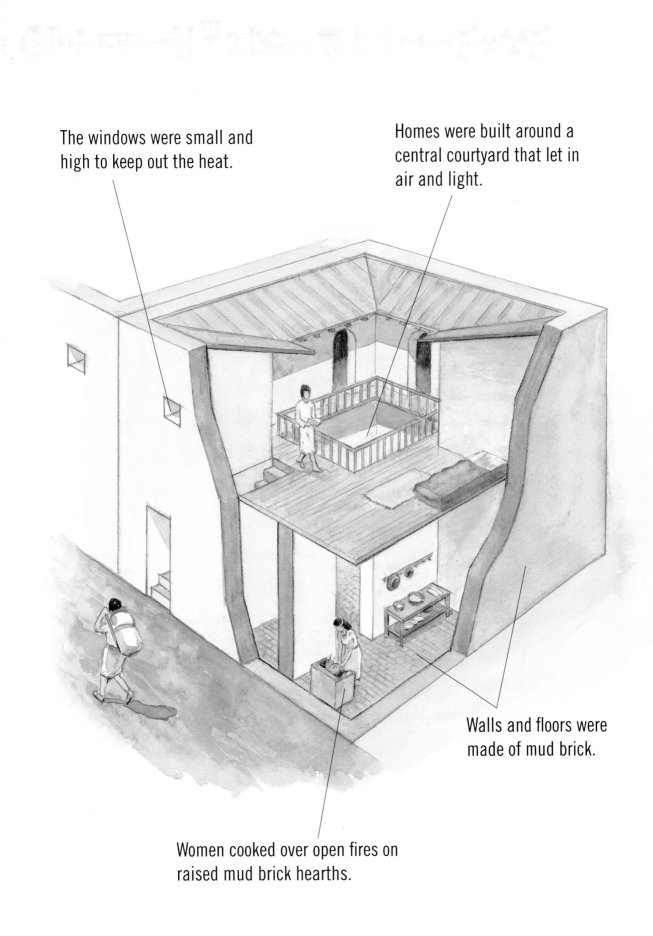

The windows were small and high to keep out the heat.

Homes were built around a central courtyard that let in air and light.

Walls and floors were made of mud brick.

Women cooked over open fires on raised mud brick hearths.

Families

In Sumer, parents arranged their children's marriages. Men worked and made the family decisions. Women took care of the home and raised the children. Some women did run businesses. These were usually widows who took over the family business when their husbands died. But girls did not go to school. Their mothers taught them how to run a home.

Some boys learned to read and write so they could become **scribes**. Scribes were important in the government of a **city-state**. It took years to learn the symbols, words, and phrases of Sumerian writing by heart. The boys also studied math, geography, and astronomy.

This statue shows an important Sumerian man, who may have been a teacher. Sumerian teachers were always men.

Going to school cost money, so only boys from wealthy families could go. The rest learned how to do their fathers' jobs. There were many different jobs available in the cities. Some potters, metalworkers, jewelers, and other craft workers worked for themselves. Others worked for the **temples**, the king, or wealthy families. In the countryside, boys grew up to be farmers or fishers.

Wealthy families might have **slaves** working for them. Slaves were usually prisoners who had been captured in war, but some crimes had slavery as a punishment. Slaves could be freed at any time.

Today people can see sculptures made by Sumerian metalworkers in museums.

Rich and important women wore expensive jewelry. This jewelry was found in Ur, in a queen's grave.

Sumerians made clothes from finely woven linen and wool. They looped and bunched the thread. In carvings from the time, it looks like tufts of sheepskin and fleece. Working people wore simple clothes that were easy to move in. Rich, important people wore longer clothes made from more expensive cloth. They wore leather shoes instead of **reed** sandals.

Early Sumerian men wore skirts that reached from the waist to the knee. They shaved their heads and faces. Women wore layered skirts and covered their heads and upper bodies with shawls. They put their long hair up in complicated hairstyles.

Later, the styles changed. Men wore a **tunic** or a longer skirt. Some of them grew beards and long hair. Women wore straight skirts or long tunics.

This statue of a woman shows the complicated loops of thread used to make clothes. The woman is wearing a skirt and shawl. Her feet are bare.

Writing and Calendars

This clay tablet is covered with cuneiform symbols. The symbols show a list of sheep and goats traded from one person to another.

The Sumerians were the first people to develop a written language. At first, they used pictures. The first use of pictures was on small carved seals that were used to make marks in soft clay.

In about 3300 BCE the Sumerians began using symbols instead of pictures. They used a wedge-shaped **stylus** to press the symbols into flat pieces of clay. This type of writing was called cuneiform. At first, Sumerians used writing to keep records. But by 2800 BCE the Sumerians had also started to write down stories, prayers, history, and songs.

The Sumerians needed calendars to keep track of when the rivers would flood, when to plant and **harvest** crops, and when special **festivals** for the gods should be held. They had two seasons, summer and winter. They divided the year up into 12 months of 29 or 30 days. All **city-states** used the same system, but some of them used different names for the months.

The Sumerians divided the day into two twelve hour blocks, like we do, but their days ran from one sunset to the next. They told time by using pots with the hours marked on them. The pots were filled with water that dropped slowly away through a hole in the side. The level of the water told you what time it was.

PICTOGRAM MEANING	3500 BCE	2500 BCE	1800 BCE	900 BCE	700 BCE
HEAD					
STREAM					
DRINK					

The diagram above shows how Sumerian writing changed from pictures to symbols.

Free Time

Music, singing, and dancing were all important to the Sumerians, both for everyday life and for religious **ceremonies**. They had several kinds of musical instruments, including harps, lyres, drums, pipes, and tambourines. Some people were trained as musicians, but many ordinary people could play an instrument.

The Sumerians also played board games. The most famous board game of all was found in the Royal Tombs of Ur. Archaeologists have found a written description of the game and have discovered how it may have been played. (An archaeologist is a person who studies people and objects from the past.)

This lyre would have been used in the home of a king or a very rich man.

The Royal Game of Ur was found in a grave from about 2600 BCE.

The different patterns on the squares meant different things. Some squares were lucky, and they helped a player who landed on them. Others were unlucky.

Both players shared the center strip. When counters were here they could be taken by the other player.

The winner was the player who got all their counters to this square first.

The game was a race. The players started here and followed the red and blue dotted lines.

These counters were used to race around the board.

End of Empire

Ur became an **empire** around 2125 BCE. The king of Ur ruled all of Sumer. But by 2020 BCE Sumer had broken up into **city-states** again. At first Sumerian kings ruled these city-states. In 2004 BCE, the Elamite people from the east captured Ur and destroyed the city. Sumer became a land of city-states that were ruled by different peoples. It was the end of the Sumerian period. It was not until 1792 CE that this part of Mesopotamia was united again. The Babylonian leader Hammurabi ruled the area at that time.

The Elamites did not rule Sumer for long. They were driven out by the Amorites. This carving shows the taking of the city.

Glossary

bitumen tar-like material

canal deep ditch filled with water

ceremony set of acts that has religious meaning

city-state city and the nearby towns, villages, and land controlled by the ruler

empire group of territories or lands controlled by one country

festival time of celebration

harvest season when crops are gathered; or, to gather a crop

irrigation bringing water to crops

ointment greasy medicine that is used on the skin

poultice medicine and herbs that are heated and placed on the body

reed tall grass that grows in wet areas

scribe person whose job is to read, write, and keep records

shrine special place for worshipping

slave person belonging to someone else who is forced to work without pay

stylus pointed instrument used for writing on clay tablets

temple building for religious worship

tunic knee-length belted garment

ziggurat pyramid-shaped temple made of layers

Find Out More

Books

Henderson, Kathy. *Lugalbanda: The Boy Who Got Caught Up in a War.* Cambridge, Mass.: Candlewick, 2006.

Mehta-Jones, Shilpa. *Life in Ancient Mesopotamia.* New York: Crabtree, 2005.

Morley, Jacqueline. *You Wouldn't Want to Be a Sumerian Slave!* Danbury, Conn.: Franklin Watts, 2007.

Websites

www.ancientscripts.com/sumerian.html
This website explores the Sumerian writing system.

www.historyforkids.org/learn/westasia/history/sumerians.htm
A website that brings ancient history to kids.

Index